DIRECTING
BUSINESS

MOVIES AND MANAGEMENT
LESSONS FOR DREAMERS

FROM A BUSINESS LEADER + MOVIE ENTHUSIAST

LAKSHMI
NARAYANA

ISBN

Hardcase 979-8-88815-621-6
Paperback 979-8-88749-846-1

Table of Contents

Acknowledgments

Thanks to everyone on the Notion Press team who helped me in getting a quality product out. Special thanks to Hema Priyadharshni, the Publishing Manager; Anupama Rajesh, the Editor, and John Jasso, the cover designer and Swetha Muthukrishnan, the publishing consultant.

And, my deepest gratitude to all those who helped shape my career so far – my colleagues, bosses and clients.

Disclaimer

The use of masculine or feminine genders or titles in this book shall be construed to include both genders and not as a sex limitation. The author represents this book to everyone irrespective of all genders and differences.

Introduction

My first teachers in the world

My introduction to the world of business and entrepreneurship began at a very early age, like in the movie **The Goodfellas**. The only difference was that my neighbourhood was not gangster-infested. It was a nice little middle-class area with people trying to make an honest buck. It was adjacent to the main road which was full of shops and general hustle-bustle. All that we needed for our household was within walking distance and every trip was an opportunity to pocket small delights like a *chikki* worth 5 paise or the slightly more expensive éclairs worth 35 paise.

When I was sent on last-minute errands such as buying grocery items or picking up cigars for my grandfather, I would make it a point to visit a particular shop. There were three big shops in the vicinity—a nice Marwari family shop that stocked pretty much everything, a better decorated and nicely lit store beside it with a smart aleck at the helm of affairs and another store with a scary guy who frowned at everyone and seemed to be angry at everyone for no reason. (We nicknamed him *shidku*, loosely translated as 'forever angry' in Kannada).

You might have already gathered from my adjectives that my preferred destination was the Marwari shop. It was the epitome of the so-called General and *Kirana* Stores, the term used for a mini supermarket in earlier times. Everything was stocked in two levels within the shop. It was not the variety, but how people treated me there that attracted me to the shop. The people in the shop included an old man wearing the traditional attire including slip-on shoes who talked non-stop and yet managed to wish me every time I was there, his son who was the defacto head of the shop managing the cash counter, handing me the change and two assistants who mysteriously appeared from above and below, to hand out the items in my list.

All of them treated me like a customer and not like a mere seven-year-old. Even when the store was crowded, the rule of first-come-first-serve was not ignored even once. (There were no tokens but the watchful eyes of the talkative old man made up for them. *"Look, this kid came in first,"* was all he had to say if it came to that). One of the assistants would make harmless fun of my little stutter once in a while, but it never rubbed me the wrong way. The other two shops did everything to the contrary without any intent. For instance, when I told the fancy store guy to give me the item correctly so that I didn't have to make repeat visits, he would say, *"You are a boy and so you can run back and forth ten times"* or something similar. No wonder, I shopped there only when there was an emergency. It was the same with the *shidku*. This was despite the fact that his shop was on the same side of the road as our house and just a few blocks away.

So, these shops made up somewhat of a trinity for me. The *shidku* was like the world-averse Shiva and whom I avoided, the condescending and fancy Brahma whom I visited only when I had to and the world-wise and genial Vishnu whom I loved to frequent. Thus began the education of **The Matrix** around me and it continues even today.

Why movies?

The first movie I saw, according to my mother, was a Telugu film called **Bangaru Babu** when I was a month old. I know, technically I cannot say that I saw it, but you get the drift. As years went by, my interest in movies increased manifold and I have lost count of the number of movies I have watched to date. Actually, I have been tracking the movies and TV shows I have been watching for the last few years in an excel sheet. I am even trying to put together a list of movies prior to that...but it's a work in progress.

Somewhere in the late 90s, I realized that movies are more than just entertainment. As my interest in management and leadership grew, so did my observations about movies and the concepts portrayed in them. Maybe this also helped me rationalize my madness about movies and watching at least one film a day.

"Hey! movies offer a nice education too," I constantly told myself and others. *"You can correlate management concepts with movies or certain scenes,"* remained my constant refrain. I do stay away from referring to movies like Peter Jackson's **Bad Taste,** though it is not a bad movie for a debutant director. But from a management standpoint? Not a good choice!

Anyways, the point I am trying to make is that there are movies, especially the old ones, that offer quite a few pointers to people at various levels of management and leadership. Whether you are running your own business or aspire to run one, whether you are in the corporate world and aim to rise higher on the ladder, you will find quite a few movies that almost act as practical case studies and supplement your regular education. You will find more about these during the course of this book.

So, I hope I have made my point about why I chose movies. If not, I hope you will agree to the premise either in the middle or at the end of this book.

Why read this book? Who should read this book?

This book is not meant to teach you management skills or how to run a business. It also does not teach you how to be an entrepreneur. Think of this book as a reminder of some of the best techniques you already know. If this book urges you to learn more and watch more movies from a learning point of view, I feel that it has achieved its purpose.

It All Begins with a Pitch

"It's possible isn't it?"

– Henry Fonda in
The 12 Angry Men

A nagging question. An inexplicable restlessness. A recurring dream. A remote possibility. Against all odds. Does this sound familiar? Then you might be an entrepreneur in the making.

In the movie 12 Angry Men, Henry Fonda is a different kind of entrepreneur. He is a soft seller, the dangerous kind as a fellow juror points out in exasperation when he misses his ball game. But what's he selling? A glimmer of reasonable doubt that if all of them agree, it can potentially save the accused from hanging. How he builds a consensus amongst a motley group of individuals coming from various backgrounds, how he carries the beacon of logic across the volatile sea of emotions and prejudices, and how he painstakingly garners the support of the others one after another is a must-watch for any aspirant in business or entrepreneurship. When his mission in the movie is accomplished, he walks out nonchalantly, just in time to make his name known for the first time.

There's a similar scene in the movie **The Untouchables** when Eliott Ness (Kevin Kostner) walks out of his office after putting Al Capone behind bars and a reporter asks him what would he do if prohibition were lifted. *"I will have a drink,"* he says. Coming from the hero who just risked everything to go against prohibition-law breakers, it is a great watch.

We first pitch something to ourselves before we do it to the outside world. It gets refined when it hits the real world, but a semblance of it begins with us. For instance, Bill Gates might have thought personal computers are the future and it might lead to "A computer on every desk and in every home."

Great pitches often branch off into brand positioning statements or even tag lines and sometimes even a vision for the company. A vision has to appeal to a lot of people, so why not pitch it to yourself first? Why not make it attractive to yourself in the first place? When you do that and answer any related question in plain speak, your pitch begins to attract like-minded people (in the initial phase very few) and the wheels are set in motion.

The Untouchables has one such classic scene where Malone meets Ness for the second time. Ness initially fails to convince Malone to go with his intent to capture Al Capone. But surprisingly Malone turns up at Ness's office and insists on meeting outside as the walls have ears.

Malone: [talking privately in a church] You said you wanted to get Capone. Do you really wanna get him? You see, what I'm saying is, what are you prepared to do?
Ness: Anything within the law.
Malone: And then what are you prepared to do? If you open the ball on these people, you must be prepared to go all the way. Because they're not gonna give up the fight, until one of you is dead.
Ness: I want to get Capone! I don't know how to do it.
Malone: You wanna know how to get Capone? They pull a knife, you pull a gun. He sends one of yours to the hospital, you send one of his to the morgue. That's the Chicago way! And that's how you get Capone. Now do you want to do that? Are

> *you ready to do that? I'm offering you a*
> *deal. Do you want this deal?*
> *Ness: I have sworn to capture this man with*
> *all legal powers at my disposal and I will*
> *do so.*
> *Malone: Well, the Lord hates a coward [jabs*
> *Ness with his hand, and Ness shakes it]*
> *Malone: Do you know what a blood oath is,*
> *Mr. Ness?*
> *Ness: Yes.*
> *Malone: Good, 'cause you just took one.*

At the end of the above conversation, a simple yet genuine pitch, *"I have sworn to capture this man with all legal powers at my disposal and I will do so,"* results in the joining of the second member of the gang, a gang so remote from the corrupt police force that it is known as the squad of The Untouchables.

Pitches are most often quite simple. A pitch by definition is simple to understand. It is the environment onto which it is projected that makes it difficult. *"I want Al Capone"* is a pitch that is next to impossible because of the power Al Capone wields in the real world. Similarly, the simple pitch made by the juror dressed in white for a brief discussion before passing a guilty verdict becomes that much more difficult when presented with the objective of facing 11 other jurors who are hard like stone, immersed in their worlds of strong perception.

Not all pitches need to accomplish herculean tasks like that of Elon Musk's 'affordable space travel.' But invariably a pitch has an element of difficulty in it, otherwise what is there for a future entrepreneur to work against?

Pitches often disguise themselves as dreams or questions. Joseph Campbell in his terrific book **The Hero with a Thousand Faces** talks about a typical journey of a hero from a dream to redemption. George Lucas used this theory to good effect in **Star Wars**. Why am I here? What should I do? While these remain nagging questions, a haunting dream of a new destination pushes things forward. There comes a moment when we 'Feel the force.'

We pitch all along. A pitch is not just limited to the genesis of a company or the start of an endeavor. You need it at every stage and in a variety of situations. Whether it is presenting to investors or trying to hire a star employee or warding off a scandal in a press meet, a simple and effective pitch is the way to go in each case.

How can you come up with the best pitch? You don't try. Version one first flows from your knowledge and conviction. Subsequent versions can change, sometimes even minutes before delivering it. Once it is out in the world, it keeps changing even more. As we keep perfecting it, doors keep opening and we move forward.

Financials and Annual Reports

"You've copied me on the company's financial statements for 17 years. You just assumed I couldn't read."

**– David (Greg Kinnear)
in Sabrina (1995)**

True. Anyone who can read and keep at it for some time will find financials to be a great source of learning. How a company performs in its last quarter or financial year will help us decode its success and learn from its mistakes. One can gather quite a bit from the write-off sections, where a few millions are just washed away as an investment in a product that didn't take off or as a huge expenditure against a project that did not materialize. Here's a hilarious conversation between Kramer and Jerry in **Seinfeld's The Package**.

> *"It's a write-off for them."*
> *"How is it a write-off?"*
> *"They just write it off."*
> *"Write it off what?"*
> *"Jerry, all these big companies, they write off everything."*
> *"You don't even know what a write-off is."*
> *"Do you?"*
> *"No, I don't."*
> *"But they do. And they're the ones writing it off."*
> *"I wish I had the last twenty seconds of my life back."*

Anyone aspiring to be an entrepreneur or run a business should read annual reports too. They are like mini autobiographies covering the year that has elapsed. Just like an autobiography, they can afford to neither exaggerate the progress nor belittle the achievements. For an investor, they contain plain speak about the financials yet give a perspective about the company's hits and misses.

Even if you do not understand everything in it, you should pick up a few and start reading them. Back in the olden days before the internet took over, many would buy a share or two in a company just to receive its annual report. Now, you do not have to be an investor to read an annual report or to check the financials of a company. All you have to do is to visit its corporate website. Every publicly traded company has to keep these documents available online and many private companies do it too, to provide transparency.

CEOs of companies, both big and small, use these reports to convey an important message to their investors. People are all ears when industry leaders like Warren Buffet or Jeff Bezos spill their thoughts in the letters addressed to stakeholders. Maybe such letters also help them stay true to their course. Recently, in one such communication, Jeff Bezos referred to a decade-old letter and stressed the importance of the themes Amazon adheres to.

There are companies like annualreports.com that even evaluate and rank the best annual reports every year using a variety of criteria like communication and style, operations and sustainability, strategy and leadership, figures and financials, and investors and governance.

So, what are you waiting for? The best things in life are free. Start digging into annual reports of your choice in both the industry you operate and the ones you would like to benchmark against or just something you pick up randomly. Look up the terms you don't understand on the internet and keep exploring.

My favourite annual report over the years has been that of Infosys and I have been following it for over a decade (without owning a single share, of course) and very recently, that of Akshaya Patra Foundation (where I intend to be an active donor soon). Now I plan to expand my choice and keep adding companies to my watchlist as per annualreports.com or similar websites.

Business Plan...Do You Need One?

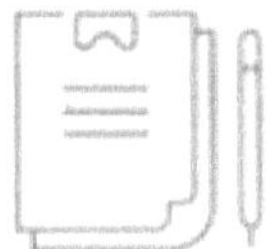

In 1999, I attended a meeting at a reputed finance firm in Manhattan, along with my boss, who was in his element that day and at his talkative best. He delivered a great pitch and the finance guy was all praise for his business model and even said that if it were up to him, he would quit his current job and join us. After a round of coffee and water (my boss was a tea-totaller, oops, water-totaller at that time), the subject of a business plan cropped up.

"Just share a copy and I will work on the rest," said the finance guy.

My boss then dropped the bombshell.

> *"I set up a 1000 Cr+ business but never had a plan till date. I get the idea and my finance guy puts it in a proper format."*

Thankfully, the person understood my boss's viewpoint as an entrepreneur raring to go and worked with us from scratch. My boss spoke for another half hour, explained what he was trying to do and simply said, *"Lakshmi will take care of the rest."*

That 'rest' took us a month and the guy was patience personified in dealing with my ignorance (the fact that we were paying him an excellent hourly rate, helped in good measure). We came up with a business plan that was suitable for investors and the company took off to the next level.

A year later, in India, just before the company went public, I repeated the exercise with a local company for the research and the outline and then employed a leading consulting firm to convert it into an investor-friendly format.

Over the years, I have worked on several business plans, either to raise money at various stages of the company's growth or to simply put in business ideas to denote the way forward.

So, do I see the need for a business plan? Does an entrepreneur need it? How actively should he be involved in the making of it?

To begin with, let's look at it from the entrepreneur's viewpoint. In this case, my ex-boss. His logic was simple in starting a new business and he distilled it into three questions. Mind you, the answers for these may come out as simple yes or no, but there is a lot of work that happens in the background which is more or less internalized.

Scenario 1

1. Is the market good enough and growing for this product/service?
2. Who are the current competitors?
3. If they can do it, can I do it too? How do I go about it?

For an entrepreneur, out of the three questions above the answer to question 3 is a yes by default. How big the competitor is doesn't matter to him as long as a strategy is firmed up in his mind.

Scenario 2

This can encompass a different set of questions.

1. Which pain point is this new product or service addressing? Which existing business segment is it disrupting?
2. How big is the market for it?
3. I can do it. How do I go about it?

The dangerous or the riskiest scenario and of course the most rewarding is when the following questions are asked or rather not asked.

Scenario 3

1. I know this is a great product/service and customers will buy it. (Is this a great product/service, will the customers buy it?)
2. I have to create a market for it. (Will there be a market for it?)
3. I can do it. How do I go about it?

In a typical business plan, the first two questions are answered in detail. As you have to put together one anyway, you can either decide to use the business plan at the start of the new business or at a later stage. As you start moving from one venture to another, you will find that this exercise is inevitable. But you can still keep the initial thinking to a set of few questions if not just the three mentioned above. An entrepreneur should always drive the plan and make sure his ideas are intact. Also, depending on the nature of the business, the extent of the effort involved in the business plan will change.

Let's look at interesting examples from a few TV series to illustrate three scenarios and how the characters approached them. Who better to get the point across than Mr.Walter White?

Walter White leads a rather sedate life till he stumbles into the meth business. Actually, lung cancer hits him first and upsets his apple cart.

Until he arrives on the scene, the purification of the drug meth was considered impossible beyond a certain point. As soon as he manages to do it and realizes that he has a great product, he learns about the business quickly and expands like there was no tomorrow. (Well, that was the thought in the beginning anyway as he had lung cancer and his prognosis was bad). So, the moment he answered the three questions in Scenario 3, he literally became the Steve Jobs of the meth business. There are more details in the next chapter, but for now, let's look at other examples.

In the movie **Pirates of Silicon Valley**, Bill Gates and Steve Jobs are shown pursuing Scenario 3 in their own way. Both are convinced about the future of the personal computer and start building a market while the big boys in the industry underestimate its potential. Whether the movie is factual or not, it is good fun to see the exaggerated scenes that nevertheless show their entrepreneurial spirit. Some interesting scenes include the first meeting at Microsoft headquarters and Steve Jobs hopping from bank to bank in search of a loan.

Tony Montana in **Scarface** (1983) follows Scenario 1. A Cuban refugee, who has nothing to lose and nothing in hand, rises to become a powerful drug kingpin. In the film, he is shown as a big proponent of the philosophy, 'If they can do it, I can do it too.' Whatever connections he lacks, he makes up with his fearlessness and aggression.

Even if you are not a Tony Montana or Walter White, figuring out which business to run and tackling it head-on, obviously doesn't need much of a plan. Once you internalize all the details and make up your mind, you are good to go.

But, for us mortals, as the company progresses, a business plan always comes into play. So, be prepared for the eventuality. Keep the questions simple and get a move on. Let this rolling stone of business gather moss. Allow everything to converge into a business plan. Make it work for you and the outside world and maybe, dress up for the occasion too. The short conversation from Pirates of Silicon Valley below illustrates this.

> *Steve Wozniak: Where's your beard?*
> *Steve Jobs: In the bathroom sink. I shaved it off.*
> *Steve Wozniak: Well, how come?*
> *Steve Jobs: 'Cause banks don't like beards.*

The Itch of an Entrepreneur

"You see things; you say, 'Why?' But I dream things that never were; and I say 'Why not?' "

– George Bernard Shaw

An entrepreneur, especially a first-generation entrepreneur is characterized by a sense of restlessness and a sense of urgency that often stems from his ability to spot an opportunity that others seem to ignore or don't see as being very important.

"A hero ventures forth from the world of common day into a region of supernatural wonder: fabulous forces are there encountered and a decisive victory is won: The hero comes back from this mysterious adventure with the power to bestow boons on his fellow man."

– Joseph Campbell,
The Hero with a Thousand Faces

An entrepreneur's journey into uncharted waters is no different from that of a hero. For many first-generation entrepreneurs, it all begins with a deep desire, a deep unsettling desire. Most of the time, the objective is to either change their lifestyle or change the world around them. For many, it is the latter.

Once the desire is strong enough, the entrepreneur sets out to pick up the required skills and then finally implement them. In Sanskrit, this is brilliantly captured as *iccha sakthi* (power to imagine/desire), *gnana sakthi* (power of knowledge/skills) and *kriya sakthi* (power to execute). An entrepreneur has to keep his eye on all three, not only at the start of the career but also throughout his journey.

As an entrepreneur, you face challenges daily. Whether it feels like it or not, the outing is not unlike the hero's journey depicted by Joseph Campbell. Here are some selected steps from the hero's journey that are very relevant to an entrepreneur.

1. Call to adventure
2. Meeting the mentor/s
3. Test/s, allies, enemies
4. Ordeal/s, death, rebirth
5. Return with the elixir

While the call to adventure (the reason for doing it all, that deep desire) is something that arises from within and usually beckons you to new worlds, the rest is what an entrepreneur does there. For any entrepreneur, every day is a learning experience. So each day is like a new world. Meeting the mentors and engaging in tests is what gets him ready for the biggest ordeal. When he comes out of it, he has something big to offer himself or the outside world. His offering is sometimes internal (a stroke of wisdom) or external (a terrific deal or happy employees who just exercised their stock options).

If you reflect on these steps, it also gives a sense of how you must manage your time. Some time for quiet reflection (for clarity and rekindling the deep desire), some time for learning (yourself and with mentors), some time for tests (planned and unplanned) and some time for the big ordeal (hopefully not every day and you cannot plan that anyway). The result of it all is that you feel energized and rewarded enough to get back to the world as it is a never-ending journey.

> *"I don't want anything to happen to him while my mother's alive."*
>
> **– Michael Corleone to Al Neri in The Godfather**

Let's look at a few movies that throw some light on each of the steps above. In the classic **The Godfather II**, the entrepreneurial journey of Vito Corleone begins when he is displaced from his home town and gives shape to his deep desire to make a name for himself. The Godfather also provides excellent examples of tests that decide the protagonists' allies and enemies, either of their own making or those that they face. While loyalty is the key to the family staying together, the protagonists do not hesitate to take tough decisions even when the person is a part of the family. While we cannot do something drastic like Michael Corleone (Al Pacino), like sending Fredo (John Cazale) or Tessio (Abe Vigoda) to the gallows, we can still remember that it is important for entrepreneurs and managers to take decisive action and become wise.

> *"I wish I could tell you that Andy fought the good fight, and the sisters let him be. I wish I could tell you that - but prison is no fairy-tale world. He never said who did it, but we all knew."*

– Red

In the movie **The Shawshank Redemption**, Andy Dufresne (Tim Robbins) is pushed into a new world but he makes his own life there. As he starts helping people, he makes new allies and enemies. Every day is a test for him and somehow he picks himself up from dirt every time he falls. He becomes an entrepreneur who is constantly on the lookout for new opportunities to change his life and that of people around him, and every time he does that his life takes a different turn.

Initially, he helps the prison guard, and the same guard rescues him from the dreaded sisters' gang. When he begins to help the warden with his work, he gets the independence to build the best prison library ever. He deals with the biggest ordeal when he realizes that the warden will never let him go, but he comes out of the tunnel (rather literally) into a new life. In the end, the hero's rewards are a life-long experience, a great friend and of course, his severance pay from the warden.

Is My Business Doing Ok?

"What gets measured, gets managed."

– Peter Drucker

Am I doing ok? When we are posed with this seemingly harmless question, we might revert to a perfunctory yes or no, without giving it too much thought. But a doctor approaches it differently. He may first collect vital stats and then if required, dig deeper with a battery of tests to further ascertain your physical and then, mental health. At the end of it all, you will receive a declaration of sorts about your health. So much for your simple 'yes' or 'no' tactic.

What about applying the doctor-like approach to business? If you are running a business of your own, or even manage a team of your own, you need to become your own doctor and prepare a list of health indicators and layer them. You need to identify metrics at various levels and work on the presentation/display. In the world of data analytics, such effort is often translated into complex reports and dashboards. Companies like Intel and GE have elaborate programs put in place where a collection of data about metrics and reports about them are nothing short of a religion.

But it doesn't have to be all that complicated and prolonged. One also need not leave such philosophy at the door, assuming that it is suited for companies of a certain size or industry. Many business leaders have shown the way via simple techniques. For instance, a famous Birla at one time used to just track the profit for one cement bag and leave out the rest. Same with the owner of the local *kirana* store, who can judge his shop's health by the money left in his cash box at the end of the day. It's not just the Tatas or Birlas or your local store, even the mafia knows to track its business health. Sample this.

In a scene from the movie The Untouchables, Al Capone (Robert De Niro) is served a royal breakfast along with a newspaper and a ledger, both giving him an indication as to how his previous day went. Robert De Niro, while puffing a cigar, laughs at Eliot Ness's discomfort captured on the front page of the paper. He is happy with how the previous day turned out and he could surely hope for a good day in the present with all the muscle power at his disposal. But what about regular guys like us?

The health of your business can be measured based on certain pre-decided indicators. These indicators are more commonly known as metrics and can be classified into output metrics and input metrics. Output metrics, as the name suggests, are tracked but there is not much that you can do to change them e.g. the profit at the end of the quarter or the cash in the box or the closing price of the stock at the end of the day. Input metrics, on the contrary, are the ones that lead to the output. You can track them and tweak the effort you put in to get a better output. Simply put, if you produce more cement bags and if you sell them at a certain price, your output or profit will be more.

An analysis of metrics over time, in a comprehensive manner (dashboard) and at various levels (cascading) of the business can offer further insight into the health of your business. Let's look at each of these in a little more detail.

- **Historical data**: It's about what happened before—a minute ago, a day ago or a year ago. How far into the past you want to go is often dictated by your business. If you are a media house, for example, you would probably keep track of everything you can from the past. On the other hand, if you are a stockbroker, you would limit yourself to the life cycle of a particular stock or a certain industry. This element of data collection is very helpful in learning and knowledge building.

- **Real-time data**: It's all about what's happening now to your chosen set of metrics. It's a bit like my version of an ICU i.e. Intensive Control Unit where you clearly see what's going on, right away. In the case of the media house, it is the news ticker or the breaking news that's just in. For the stockbroker, it is the current price of his chosen stock.

- **Dashboard / Scorecard / Mission Control Center**: Each of these is a centralised display of various metrics for the key stakeholders to track their progress and make any course corrections. The dashboard is a fairly simple projection of output metrics like the one in your cars. The scorecard is more detailed and shows cascading metrics (the ability to drill down to more metrics). A mission control center, as the name suggests, is taken from the space launch stations where several metrics are tracked visually and in real-time

(As Ed Harris intones in **Apollo 13**, *"Failure is not an option."*)

- **Cascading metrics and balanced scorecard**: The balanced scorecard concept was created by Robert S. Kaplan and David P. Norton and offers a detailed display of all metrics—financial and non-financial—linked to the strategy. Such metrics cascade down from the high-level strategy to execution at various levels. There are several books and training courses to provide in-depth guidance about its implementation.

Let's condense all the above into a few simple steps.

1. Translate the corporate vision into a set of goals for the business/team
2. Come up with initiatives/themes aligning with the vision
3. Create projects that fall under the initiatives
4. Prepare a set of metrics to track—input and output—for every project
5. Display the progress for everyone to see and change course

In many companies vision statements are displayed prominently and so are those of the individual departments or teams. But most often, specifics in terms of goals and achievements are not shared, leaving vision statements as mere wall decorations.

So, how do we go about having a vision and then making the team understand what they are supposed to achieve? Let's look at two all-time classic movies—**The Great Escape** (1963) and **Seven Samurai** (1954).

In the movie Seven Samurai, the key members of the leadership team understand the nature of the mission clearly (dangerous, odds stacked against, no pay and only food) and the vision (freeing the village from bandits before harvest). The leader breaks the vision into two—to kill the bandits in the immediate future and train the villagers to prepare them for any future attacks. He then sets initiatives that align with the vision, like defending the terrain or preparing for the attack. Further, smaller projects are assigned to individual leaders (training the villagers, digging water pits, building barricades, etc). When the battle begins, a simple chart with all the bandits depicted as circles is used to track their killing (key output metric) during the fights.

The Great Escape is another interesting film with a clearly defined vision for all the prisoners of war by allied forces. For a successful escape, they must create confusion and chaos during the escape attempts.

"All rotten eggs in a single basket," comments the head of the prison camp as a group of seasoned

escape artists plans the most audacious escape attempt ever.

The leader, Big X/Bartlett (Richard Attenborough) quickly assembles the team and creates projects for each initiative related to the escape, like the forgery of identity papers, properly tailored clothes, digging tunnels, disposal of the dirt, scrounging from soldiers, surveillance mechanisms, etc. Once these are in place, he pushes the teams to achieve their best, with clear metrics in place. He starts with a never-before achieved output metric of prison escape and scales up all other projects to meet the same goal.

> *Hilts: How many you taking out?*
> *Bartlett: Two hundred and fifty.*
> *Hilts: Two hundred and fifty?*
> *Bartlett: Yeh.*
> *Hilts: You're crazy. You oughta be locked up. You, too. Two hundred and fifty guys just walkin' down the road, just like that?*

Mr. X also plans for redundancy and digs three tunnels just in case the goons (German guards) find out. He conducts frequent secret meetings to share the progress (one cannot set up a chart or dashboard for metrics in a prison camp) and enlist new people like Hilts (Steve McQueen) to take up suicidal missions.

Speaking of the mission control center and the beauty of managing a whole business from it, the best example is the space research organization from where the concept itself has been taken. Apollo 13, the movie directed by Ron Howard, is a fascinating display of how a set of people manage a mission even when they are thousands of miles away from each other. The output metric is changed midway and the main initiative becomes the safe return of the crew. As Flight Director Gene Kranz (Ed Harris) intones, *"Failure is not an option,"* the rest of the team works on projects to reverse engineer the path back home. Each project's output metric becomes the input metric for the final goal. A neat depiction of projects that can be nested to meet the outcome, like cascading metrics.

So, whether you are managing a business or a team, taking the **Vision>Goals>Projects>Metrics** approach will hold you in good stead. It is better not to go overboard with metrics. In the beginning, keep it simple and expand as you go along. Let the team know how the success is quantified and make this data available to everyone. Here's to hoping that the health of your business is in your hands and doesn't need any external doctors.

How to Hire Your Gunmen?

Sotero: There's one - look at the scars on his face!

Hilario: The man for us is the one who GAVE him that face.

Chris: Hey, you learn fast.

So goes the conversation between a seasoned gun-man, Chris (Yul Brynner) and three gullible farmers whom he has just agreed to help out on an important mission. The dialogue above is a great pointer for hiring, don't you think?

The Magnificent Seven (1960) is a fantastic film about how seven different individuals come together to rescue a farming village from deadly bandits. A John Sturges-helmed remake of the evergreen classic, Akira Kurosawa's Seven Samurai, it simplifies the original film to make it palatable for a wider audience. But it still leaves enough on the table for management folks to feast upon.

The situation of the farmers in this movie is similar to that of first-generation entrepreneurs who are starting their venture (but with no bandit gang leader Calvera after them, of course). These entrepreneurs are good at what they do and might be even well experienced in the product or service space they intend to operate in. But they have just realized they can't do it all on their own and need 'people.'

I encountered a similar situation in the USA when I took up an offer to set up an internet company from scratch, back in 1999. I quickly created an organizational chart and presented it to my investor/boss and got his approval. I thought that it would be easy from then on. I imagined that it would be similar to how things materialize out of a blueprint in the all-time great movie **Mayabazar** with a simple mantra and a magic wand. Obviously, I didn't have a magic wand, but I had a phone and I made my first call to a good friend of mine, thinking that if I just uttered the mantra of the job title (Head - Networking) and an opportunity to work out of our favourite place in the world—Hyderabad, India—he would drop everything and start the next day. Instead, at the end of a brief call, I received two questions for which I did not have a proper answer.

For a few minutes, my mind raced back in time and I recollected quite a few memorable incidents in college and the workplace, especially the late nights of internet browsing at the speed of a few pixels per minute. I brushed aside the flashback set to the sad song *'Yeh dosti hum nahi chodenge'* from the movie **Sholay** and focused on two things. First, I knocked off the subjective distraction from my mind after realizing that he was definitely not my Veeru and we were not that close, to begin with anyway. Second, I pondered over what he had asked about, the vision of the company. I realised that it made sense. Over the years, I have encountered several non-Veeru kinds of situations and I learned as I chugged along and am actually still learning. Here are the takeaways from my journey so far.

Spell out the vision of the company

It always helps to articulate a long-term view of where the company is headed and the vision of the company is (probably) just that. Depending on the seniority of the hire, your elaboration might change, but it should be a common feature in all your discussions either at the beginning or at the end of the conversation with a new hire. It also helps you to reiterate why the company exists in the first place, why all the effort matters, and how it all might add up five or ten years from now.

Make an earnest pitch, but do not exaggerate

There are times when you need to 'sell' your company to the new hire, whether it is a start-up or an established company, at various stages of the company's growth. Let the pitch be an enthusiastic one but grounded in reality, with a combination of the good as well as the hard things in the new job. For instance, a great job that involves long hours or tough customers, a job that offers stock options but low monthly payments, and so on.

Once in a while, you might have to do a completely negative pitch almost dissuading the prospect to join the company, like the scene in The Magnificent Seven where Chris tells Harry that the job is not in his league and the pay is very less. (Harry, of course, joins the team thinking that Chris is not telling him the whole deal about the gold. Was there any gold after all? Watch the movie to find out!).

What are the candidate's roots?

It always helps to get a sense of the candidate's anchor. In most cases, it is his immediate family.

When you start hiring, you will be surprised by how many of a professional's decisions are driven by his family. Right from the amount of pay they seek to the choice of job location, many factors stem from their personal world. If you are hiring at the junior level, it is not uncommon for the candidate to name his parent as the person who decided this career path for him. Know as much as you can about their background, maybe not to the extent that Sam Walton does (apparently he would even check the bank statements). The higher the hire, the deeper you need to dig.

Try to get a sense of comfort working with them

After a candidate checks all your requirements for qualifications, gauge your comfort with him. This can happen at any point during the interview. It could be the way he walked into the room or his eagerness to shake hands or start a conversation or the amount of time it takes for him to answer. As time goes by, judge how comfortable he is talking to you or how true he is to his emotions.

There is a beautiful scene in the movie The Untouchables where Eliott Ness and Malone go to recruit good apples from the tree aka the police academy, instead of the rotten ones (existing corrupt officers). After the first filtration is done, the top candidates are brought in for the interview. Malone provokes George Stone and that becomes the basis for the latter's selection. Both Malone and Ness are convinced that Stone is the guy who will fit the job's unique requirements.

So, when we talk about comfort, please understand that it's not just about you but also what the job entails and the candidate's ease of slipping into it. In a way, you are also assessing if you entrust this guy with the job, will he go all the way for the company?

Hire them for what they can be

No matter how senior or junior, your hire must always have an understanding of what he can be, and not just what he is. It is a bit tough to arrive at this when you are meeting a person for the first time. So, if need be, meet him again, preferably during a different time of the day or a different place altogether if it is possible. Simple straightforward questions like, *"Where do you see yourself in the next 3 to 5 years?"* still work for some people. But somewhere, you have to get into a conversation mode with the candidate and let him tell you his future story, however outlandish it might seem to both of you. Here lie the true answers.

Which one is right for you? Top-down hiring or bottom-up hiring

There's no doubt that top-down hiring is the best. You get the top guy first and he will play an active part in enlisting the rest or at least have some solid ideas for what they could be like. It's similar to how the farmers stumble onto Chris and he assembles the rest of the team to form The Magnificient Seven. It's usually the approach for any mission. Once you pick the leader, he, in turn, picks the team.

Sometimes it can be both. For instance, in the movie **The Guns of Navarone,** the leader is brought in first and handed over a dossier of people who will work with him. Being a seasoned veteran, Capt. Keith Mallory (Gregory Peck) knows a couple of them already and is comfortable teaming up with them, but he gets to know the rest as he goes along. In successive missions, it is a norm for a set of guys to come together for a common cause, like in the case of the **Mission Impossible** series.

Sometimes practical difficulties force the HR department or the top leaders to hire at various levels even before the heads are in place. As the team size increases or the operations grow, bringing in the management/leadership layer becomes inevitable. It is the same with a start-up that usually avoids layers until the company reaches a certain maturity and then recruits suitable candidates.

As the new age companies like Google and Facebook have shown, the managers don't necessarily just manage but chip in with individual contributions too, much like the playing captain of a cricket team or like our expert gunman Chris in The Magnificient Seven, Capt. Keith Mallory in The Guns of Navarone and Ethan Hunt in Mission Impossible.

How to reach out to the potential candidates

In the all-time bestseller **What color is your parachute?** the author advises job seekers to take approaches other than sending in resumes and waiting for the companies to respond. Similarly, when you are looking to hire for a particular role, referrals are probably the best bet. But you need to be a bit careful about the source of referral. Always check the source for his capability, and if he is qualified enough to make that referral in the first place. No matter how close the person is to you, either personally or professionally, referrals must be approached after thorough research.

Don Ward: You're firing me?
Ace Rothstein: I'm firing you. No, I'm not firing, I'm firing you, ya...
Don Ward: You might regret this, Mr. Rothstein.
Ace Rothstein: I'll regret it even more if I keep you on.

– From the movie Casino

* * *

Tom: Now your new son-in-law; give him something important?
Vito Corleone: Never. Give him a living, but never discuss the Family business with him. What else?

– From the movie The Godfather

Sometimes referrals are not presented as such and end up as obvious choices or forced recommendations such as a close relative of a board director or a son of a loyal ex-employee. Such situations require a bit of tact, unlike the resentment of Ace Rothstein towards the nephew of the County Commissioner in the movie Casino. One should employ the subtle technique of Don Sr. in 'The Godfather' where he advises Tom to give his future son-in-law a living, but never share anything important. Like always, the subtlest message is the strongest.

In the case of any referrals (both offline and online), always screen them like your regular candidates but knock off a few stages in interviewing process. For example, you can jump to the final interview instead of doing the regular rounds. But, it all depends on your comfort and the seniority of the role. You could show the same caution even if the candidates are screened through an HR firm or your internal HR or when the candidate in question is the first connection of your mentor or colleague on Linkedin.

Obviously, you can't fill all the roles without the regular hiring process of online/offline paid advertisements and the related screening process. Now and then, you might have to employ broadcast messaging to get the pool from which you have to select a candidate. In such cases, take extra care to ensure that the message is right and the job description is neither too long nor too short. The best way to do this is by first getting the target community right. For instance, if you are looking for programmers, you are better off finding a way to target them and then detailing the opportunity rather than running a front-page advert on the offline version of 'The New York Times.' The same thing applies when you dealing with a head-hunter.

You can take a cue from The Magnificent Seven again, wherein the poor farmers find their target community by reaching the city where all the action is. Once they find Chris, they tell him what they are looking for in a few lines. All Chris had to do was ask a couple of questions to hear their earnest pitch. He then begins to act, after his memorable dialogue, "*I have been offered a lot for my work, but never everything.*"

Hope you all find your version of Chris or become a version of him and go all guns blazing! The more, the merrier. Like Uncle Sam, always wear the hiring hat. You never know what you could accomplish with a person, even though you might not be actively looking for him.

Remember the leg spinner in **Lagaan**?

Building a Team

When Lagaan was released in 2001, it created box office history and won international acclaim. It also received a lot of praise in the management circles and several articles came out on how the movie provides pointers for HR practices. The film is about a youngster who puts himself and his village in a do-or-die situation. He has to either win a cricket match or end up paying a penalty of double the taxes to the then-ruling British government. With odds stacked against him, he sets out to assemble his team from the village and in the process, discovers how the game of cricket is actually played. Some of the interesting scenes in the film feature the physically challenged outcast, his unique skill of spin bowling and how the rest come to accept him as a part of the team. Lagaan is an excellent tale about how a motley group of individuals are brought together under one umbrella, and work towards a common mission.

Most often during our professional careers, we are forced to build a team, either with members we had a say in hiring or work with the existing lot. Realistically, it is safe to assume that we are 'given' the team we need to work with. Even if we are allowed to pick a team, there are always constraints like budgets, time, etc. that force our hand, stopping us from assembling the best team.

Lee Marvin's **The Dirty Dozen** (1967) is probably one such realistic example, where a variety of individuals (convicts) are 'gifted' to an Army Major to pull off a seemingly impossible mission. So, where does he start? He bargains hard for their payoff with the powers that be and gets it. With that payoff as motivation, he begins his work.

Motivation... what's in it for me?

This has to be the key element in getting the members of the team trained and ready for their objectives/mission. We all make sacrifices, but for what? What's in it for me? Once this is spelt out in some form it also provides a disciplinary framework for any transgressions. In the movie, Lee Marvin first makes it clear that freedom is their ultimate payoff and 'all' have to do it right to get there. With this carrot dangling before them, he has the tough task of making his team combat-ready. And every time they fail to stick to the common team goals, they are reprimanded severely. This ensures that the team is always clear about the ultimate payoff and realizes the importance of working together.

The team's payoff versus individual payoff and raising the stakes

Success and other related monetary parameters are often universal. Any incentives around them should be enough for the team to march forward, in most cases. In some scenarios though, it might not be enough. Take the case of an established company where the monetary gains are a given or a company that is already very successful with individuals doing very well (high salaries/stock options, etc.) or a not-for-profit organization where the end goals are about social transformation. Then it becomes the job of the team leader to align both goals and create a flexible structure, to goad them to work tirelessly towards the ultimate objective.

> *Hilts: How many you taking out?*
> *Bartlett: Two hundred and fifty.*
> *Hilts: Two hundred and fifty?*
> *Bartlett: Yeh.*
> *Hilts: You're crazy. You oughta be locked up. You, too. Two hundred and fifty guys just walkin' down the road, just like that?*

In the above scene from The Great Escape (1963), when Hilts (Steve McQueen) announces his plan to escape on his own, Bartlett (Richard Attenborough) skilfully asks him to be a part of a bigger mission and brings him into the fold. (Hilts voluntarily agrees after his outburst given above ☺)

In real life, when our team members are not prisoners or convicted criminals, monetary rewards are very important at an individual level. But somehow if we can create a 'team cup' at the end of it all and strike an emotional chord, building a team should be relatively easy.

In the **Ocean's Trilogy (Eleven-Thirteen)**, it is the audacity of the mission that really holds the team together than the individual share of the booty at the end. Good managers (even when not as handsome as George Clooney) can still hold a team together when there is a balance of individual and team payoff and when in doubt, they simply raise the stakes of the collective reward.

Team leader = Team member+Manager+Coach+Friend+Fiend

A team leader has to play many roles, starting from being a team member. This is quite visible in the case of the military or sports. The fact that the leader spends time in the same barrack/area as his team is in itself an indicator of a sense of commonality. If you are coaching an athlete or a cricket team, you are out there for everyone to see.

Both The Dirty Dozen and **Hoosiers** offer several examples where the leader builds trust with the team over a period of time. Some of the basic tenets that leaders follow to earn their team's loyalty are given below.

- Display transparency in dealings
- Be tough when required
- Be one with the team
- Push the common cause and mission all the time
- Put integrity before anything else
- Have fun when you can
- Bring forth innate talents in the team
- Let the team build from within (In The Dirty Dozen, Major even keeps quiet when the team bonds over an act of silly disobedience around hot water for shaving. A similar example is seen in **Chak De** when team members get into a fight in a restaurant. Even in Hoosiers a team member whom the coach just fired for not listening to him, throws a punch at the opposition team while defending the coach and the coach takes it easy)

- Fight for the team's cause (In The Dirty Dozen, the Major bargains for one last chance when the powers that be mull over scrapping the mission)
- Let go when you have to (In Hoosiers, in the time-out, the coach leaves the final decision to the team)

Work one at a time

Most often team building is associated with gatherings and events, the realm of gregarious people. But what if you are an introvert like me and you either avoid such things altogether or are there because you have to? You should make it up with one-on-one interactions and small group conversations. The more informal and candid these chats are, the better they are for you to connect with everyone. It allows you to create anchors in the team (other than you), who can hold the team together in your presence or absence. This also helps in creating the next level of leadership in the time to come.

Here are a few ideas on how to foster team spirit using small groups and individual conversations.

- In start-ups or if the team size is small, non-core work like HR, administration, etc. is often handled within the team. Assigning related tasks to individuals within the groups is a nice way to create a group leader of sorts

- Try and align individual aspirations to company goals, for example, allowing a person interested in photography to be a part of a related project
- A townhall kind of meeting is an excellent way to make a formal meeting informal. Throw in a few snacks and music and you have a party kind of atmosphere while still allowing people to speak up
- Make induction a small event. When I worked at a division of AT&T, once every month, a breakfast meeting was set up to allow the new joinees for the month to interact with the rest. When available, the division head joined in too.
- Finally, always make time for one on one conversations. Keep your door open for unannounced visits at least for some time during the day.

So, hold the team tight, and…

"Together, even the smallest can achieve the greatest goal."

– A Bug's Life

Amen!

How to Manage or How to be a Manager?

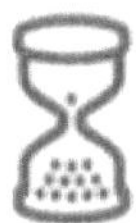

Managing others is not an easy task. But most of us have to do it in our day-to-day life. Sometimes, it is thrust upon us. It happened to me very early in my career. I was asked a head a team for a multimedia project by my super boss just a few days after joining the company. *"Why me?"* was my initial reaction, but my immediate boss assured me that not everyone gets a leadership chance like this, and often 'baptism by fire' is the best way to learn things.

> *"Management is Doing Things Right; Leadership is Doing the Right Things."*
>
> **– Peter Drucker**

Often the two terms—leader and manager—are used interchangeably. Peter Drucker summarizes it very effectively in the above quote. Just to give a little more clarity, management is all we do to get a job done, and leadership is making sure if the job itself or the method of getting it done, is right. This is probably the reason why even when people who change their path or leave their path mid-way are still hailed as great leaders. For instance, the Indian King Asoka, after the bloody win at Kalinga, wondered if it was the right thing to wage more wars. He decided to become a different kind of king by embracing Buddhism. Though he had a choice to win more kingdoms, he chose to do something else though he was very capable.

> *"A leader is one who knows the way, goes the way, and shows the way."*
>
> **– John C. Maxwell**

A leader in all probability knows what the job entails and how to get it done. In all likelihood, he might have been exposed to most or certain parts of the job in his earlier assignments. But he has something else, the ability to look beyond the job now and then. It is this trait that separates a leader from a manager. So, a leader has to be a manager, but a manager need not be a leader.

Coming back to my first managerial assignment, I had two major problems on my hand—everyone in my team was more experienced than I was and I had a tough deadline. Unfortunately, King Asoka's Buddhist option was not available to me! Thus began my journey as a manager and here are a few things I learned and a few I still aspire for.

Be transparent

> *Coach Norman Dale: Five players on the floor functioning as one single unit: team, team, team - no one more important than the other.*
>
> **– Hoosiers**

It always helps to be a straight shooter, as it helps build trust with the team. No one is an expert in everything and what you lack is supplemented by the team. So, present your strengths to the team and use them as a locus for management. In my case, I came from a content background and I understood multimedia and technology. I managed the team around it while improving my skills and expertise in new software tools.

Learning is always an option

> *Bartlett: [scoffing] What my personal feelings are is of no importance. You appointed me Big X. And it's my duty to harass, confound, and confuse the enemy to the best of my ability.*

– The Great Escape

On-the-job learning is a must for anybody and more so for a manager. Every job presents its share of challenges and new problems that need to be solved. Keeping abreast of the latest information related to the project is the way to go and one should let the team guide them in this regard. It is also possible that sometimes your ex-colleague or even an ex-boss could be a part of the team. This usually happens in a cricket team where ex-captains play under an ex-teammate. Even if this were the case, this learning approach holds the manager in good stead.

The above quote from the movie The Great Escape shows the ex-captain scenario, where Ramsey because of his injury or other reasons hands over the baton to Bartlett (Richard Attenborough) who drives the mission. Their camaraderie and collaboration are shown very well in the movie.

Overall the movie is replete with examples of management and leadership. Bartlett, though very demanding, still keeps learning from the team and makes changes accordingly.

Respect has to be earned

> *Kaffee: You don't need to wear a patch on your arm to have honor.*
> *Dawson: Ten-hut!*
> *[salutes]*
> *Dawson: There's an officer on deck.*

– A Few Good Men

It doesn't matter how experienced or how talented you are, you just can't come in and announce that everyone has to fall in line. First of all, the whole concept of a manager preaching from the pulpit and the team listening to his every word doesn't really produce results. It is only when the manager makes himself a valuable member of the team that the true team spirit kicks in. Once the team sees the manager as someone helping them individually and also achieving project goals, respect emerges automatically. It's ironic but you get to lead the team only when you work as a part of it. So find your locus and build around it. However clichéd it might sound, you have to step into your team's shoes and also allow them to do the same to be able to gain mutual respect.

In the movie A Few Good Men, there is a constant tension between the defence attorney Kaffee (Tom Cruise) who represents two marines in the court martial and the marines themselves. Kaffee is convinced that he is all they can get and tries to push his way through. In a way he is correct but that doesn't go down well with the marines. It's only towards the end when the case is solved and the marine has an epiphany about what transpired, is when that respect is born.

> *Danny: This way we never get through. We must have more wood.*
> *Willie: It's a lot of timber, Roger. Can you get it?*
> *Bartlett: We'll get it. We've gotta get it.*

Similarly, in The Great Escape, Bartlett makes it a point to know and interact with everyone in their line of work. For instance, when more wood is needed for the tunnel to hold firm, Bartlett gets a firsthand experience of the situation and promises that he will do what is needed.

Micromanagement, delegation and keeping out of someone's way

> *Bo Catlett L: Nothin' to it. All you do, you get an idea, you set down what you wanna say on paper. Then you hire somebody else to fill in the commas and shit where they belong, maybe fix up the spelling where you have tricky words. Although I've seen scripts, I know words weren't spelt right. There was hardly any commas in it at all. So I don't think that's too important. All right. You get to the end. You write in "Fade out." You done.*
> *Chili Palmer: That's it? That's all there is to it? Then what the f*** do I need you for?*

– Get Shorty

In the above beautiful scene, Chili Palmer shows us what a class act he is. Both Bo and Chili have no movie-making experience, but Chili has clarity in terms of what he cannot do and where he needs external help. In contrast, Bo thinks the other man's job is too easy and hence his fingering is definitely required. While Chili gives an 'F' to Bo, he also gives us a valuable lesson in management, to leave the right jobs to the right people and then stay out of their way.

While managing people we need to entrust tasks to people to get the job done. Sometimes it is essential to micro-manage, that is literally tell the people what to do to the extent of almost doing it. But most of the time, delegation is the best way forward. In fact, if there is only micromanagement, there is no management.

Bartlett: We'll try it first thing tomorrow.
Mac: I already have. It works.
Bartlett: Mac, this is what we'll do.

Once again Bartlett in The Great Escape shows how it is done. In the initial stages of the project, he breaks the overall project into various disciplines and immediately assigns the tasks to various teams. Once the teams are in place, he micromanages the prototypes and the initial deliverables, but once the solution comes forth he simply talks about scale-up or results, leaving the execution to the concerned person. For instance, as above, when the disposal of dirt from the tunnels poses a problem, he urges the team to find a solution. Once there is a proof of concept, he pushes for its adoption everywhere.

Conklin: We've been sleeping down there.
Believe me, we're doing everything we can.

Ward Abbott: And you don't let me know this?
Conklin: You never wanted to before.
Ward Abbott: You never made a mistake before.

– The Bourne Identity

Delegation is a trust-intensive process. We delegate to whom we trust and when we delegate, the trust builds even more. As the tasks are completed successfully, delegation can be practised at various levels and degrees of importance. Even when we delegate completely, we should still have some review mechanisms. There should be no intention to make anyone a scapegoat by showing a lack of support or being so hands-off that any failure comes as a total surprise. Delegation should not absolve the manager from his responsibility.

Be tough when you have to

There will be times when you will have to be tough, especially when dealing with talent which interferes with team goals or strategy.

Coach Norman Dale: Five players on the floor functioning as one single unit: team, team, team - no one more important than the other.

There is an excellent scene in Hoosiers where Coach Norman Dale (Gene Hackman) has to call off a key player when he doesn't conform to the team's strategy. Similarly, Captain Mallory (Gregory Peck) sidelines Brown (Stanley Baker) aka Butcher of Barcelona when he hesitates in carrying out his duties.

The key to being tough is to be consistent. As long as the team sees that everyone is treated the same way for the sake of the whole, they understand and swallow the bitter pill.

Information is on a need-to-know basis

Being transparent doesn't mean telling everyone everything. While sharing information is good, too much of it will confuse the team. The best way to enforce this is to be process driven and create an information pipeline around it.

> *[gathering wood to shore up the tunnels, Hilts removes the wooden slats from bunk beds in the sleeping area of the prisoner barracks, holding a stack of them, and walks carefully out into the hallway]*
> *Cavendish: [passes Hilts in the hallway on his way to his bunk bed] Five gold rings.*

Four calling birds - bloody singing, I've never worked so hard in all my life. Hi, Hilts!
Hilts: [turns and tries to warn him] Say, Cavendish...
Cavendish: Four calling birds, three French hens, two turtledoves, and a partridge in a pear - Alley-oop!
[Cavendish climbs to the top bunk, and vaults onto the unsupported mattress, which collapses under his weight through the bed frame, as well as the two beneath it. Hilts approaches the doorway and sees Cavendish on the floor]
Hilts: Never mind.
[Leaves]

The Great Escape offers several scenes to drive this point across including this comic situation where Capt. Hilts (Steve McQueen) decides to pick up all the wood in the bunkers for the tunnel and before he thinks it is the right time to share with the others, Cavendish (Nigel Stock) jumps into his bed only to realise that the bed wasn't there. Capt. Hilts, thinking that he should have told them earlier says, *"Never mind."* ☺

On a more serious note, throughout the team meetings, Bo Cartlett (Richard Attenborough) only discloses what is essential to the work at hand and keeps the complete picture to himself. This not only provides clarity to the team but also protects the mission, just in case someone is caught by the goons.

Expectations management

It's always important to set the expectations right with your team. Be it the deliverables from their end, or the support from your end, it's necessary to agree on them and track them from time to time. Role clarity, review meetings, status reports and written communication, all of these help in expectations management. When expectations are managed well, it prevents undue pressure and creates a healthy ambience.

Project management

> *"Turn every job into a project."*
>
> **– The Circle of Innovation by Tom Peters**

Any manager should be well versed with the principles of project management and should apply them in any situation. In fact, turning any job into a project creates the right kind of discipline in execution and also allows the manager to handle multiple projects.

MacDonald: How many men do you plan to take out, Roger?
Bartlett: Two hundred and fifty.
[Shocked stares]
Bartlett: There will be no half-measures this time, gentlemen. There will be identification papers and documents for everyone. And Griff, we'll need outfits for the lot.

Both the movies **The Bridge on River Kwai** and The Great Escape offer glimpses into project management—initiation, planning, monitoring and closure. These are evident throughout the movie during the scenes involving team meetings. The first meeting scene in The Great Escape is a classic in setting up the vision and breaking the big project into multiple smaller projects and so on. You can also see how the manager gives feedback and exhorts the team to do more.

Colonel Nicholson: Reeves, if this were your bridge, how would you get it underway?
******

Colonel Nicholson: Hughes, if this were your bridge, how would you use the men?
******

Colonel Saito: One question... can you finish the bridge in time?

> *Colonel Nicholson: Frankly, the consensus of opinion is that it's impossible... but we'll certainly give it a go. After all, we mustn't forget that we've wasted over a month through an unfortunate disagreement for which I was not to blame.*

Similarly, in The Bridge on the River Kwai, Colonel Nicholson has the first team meeting with Colonel Saito, where he clearly outlines the way forward with a perfect agenda. The scenes prior to this meeting also are quite fascinating, where Colonel Nicholson gets an overview of the terrain before taking over the project.

Project management in its simplest form is all about thinking, doing and communicating. Both these movies show us these activities in all their splendour.

Learning project management from movie producers/directors

> *"It doesn't make sense to hire smart people and tell them what to do; we hire smart people so they can tell us what to do."*

> **– Steve Jobs**

Producers and directors, who typically work on a slew of films, invariably manage a project assembly line. Right from the legendary Alfred Hitchcock to the super Steven Spielberg, they have mastered the art and craft of project management. In both sequential project management and parallel multiple project management, these people show the way. If you look at imdb.com, you will often see films assigned to a producer or director in various stages of the film like pre-production, filming, shoot, etc.

The key to making this happen is to find the right talent and empower them. Directors like George Lucas and Spielberg turn producers to talent like Robert Zemeckis (**Back To Future**) and JJ Abrams (**Star Wars: Episode VII - The Force Awakens**). They in turn hire independent and creative people in the departments of production design, cinematography, etc. and encourage them to contribute to the overall design, even though they are not experts in each domain.

Books like **Hitchcock's Notebooks: An Authorized And Illustrated Look Inside The Creative Mind Of Alfred Hitchcock** illustrate his collaborative process and how he gets the best out of his talented team. Be it breaking down the project into tasks, assigning them to individuals, seeking feedback and acting on them, making them a part of the overall vision or most importantly documenting the process, Hitchcock shows us the way.

We get to hear about adherence to the process of documentation and handling teams from Indian production houses too like Geetha Arts, Suresh Productions, etc. This could be one of the reasons why they stayed so successful over the years. After all, the biggest assets are talent and time.

Say no to projects you feel like saying no to

> *Grail Knight: But choose wisely, for while the true Grail will bring you life, the false Grail will take it from you.*

There is no harm in rejecting projects that don't fall in your scope of interest or those out of your league. Yes, you should take up new challenges and scale new heights, but you should balance your mind and heart. Most often if something doesn't 'feel' right, it ends up being wrong for you.

The same applies to situations when you have some disagreement in terms of principles. In The Bridge of River Kwai, Colonel Nicholson adamantly refuses to take up bridge construction when Colonel Saito insists that even officers have to perform manual labour. It's only when Colonel Saito relents, that he commits himself and his team to the project.

As the grail knight says, it is all about choosing wisely. In the case of the cup of Christ, one could part with their life. In the case of projects, it is your peace of mind.

Leadership in Action

"That'll do, Pig. That'll do."

Leaders come in all shapes and sizes. Arthur Hoggett (James Cromwell) in the movie **Babe** finds this out when a small piglet becomes his prize-winning pet in a sheep herding competition. What is the piglet's style of getting things done? Saying please, and requesting his team to get the job done, instead of a fiery speech from the pulpit.

Most often, we associate leaders with larger-than-life personas, with their ability to move mountains. Leaders indeed succeed in achieving great undertakings, but one cannot put all of them to the same test of comparison. Sometimes, a leader's effort is just his individual contribution, which in turn leads to something big. For instance, in the Indian epic Ramayana, a squirrel goes out of its way to help Rama in building the bridge. Rama acknowledges its small but valuable effort. When he caresses it with his fingers, the trademark stripes that we see on all squirrels today appear. Even if we discount this as a myth, this simple act of the squirrel shows that any contribution towards a bigger cause, however small it may be, can be of great importance. It also ignites everyone's spirit when another leader like Rama recognizes it. From the squirrel's viewpoint, it did something out of its character. It stepped out of its comfort zone and attempted something big, a true trait of leadership.

It makes it easy to understand leadership in general, when it is seen in the context of a team, especially in scenarios where one individual marches tens and hundreds of people on a mission. The more audacious the mission is, the more obvious the lessons are.

> *"Effective leadership is not about making speeches or being liked; leadership is defined by results not attributes."*
>
> **– Peter Drucker**

Let's take a look at the movie The Guns of Navarone, which deals with a near-impossible mission involving Capt. Keith Mallory (Gregory Peck) and his team of saboteurs. Initially, Mallory's job is limited to ferrying the team to the destination and Major Franklin (Anthony Quayle) is the leader of the pack, and hence the person responsible for achieving the result. But when Franklin is injured and limited to a stretcher, Mallory becomes the de facto leader and takes on the unenviable assignment of 'getting the job done' as he keeps saying during the movie and it is not an easy job. First, he has to believe in the job and make it somehow consistent with his character. Two, he has to focus on the job (a bloody and suicidal assignment as shown in the initial scenes). Three, he has to hold the team together, a lethal combination of strong specialists and cut-throats who are individualistic and experts. Four, he has to overcome many hurdles and think on his feet. Five, and maybe the most important of all, he must make tough decisions. Six, when it is over, he has to move on.

Miller: You're rather a ruthless character, Captain Mallory.

Leadership is all about character

Ruthless or not, leadership is all about character. Most often the word 'character' is associated with good traits or nice things. But character here refers to what one is and how consistent one is in displaying it in daily life. It is this consistency that creates a magnet around the leader and attracts both the missions and the people involved in it. The Guns of Navarone does this beautifully by presenting the multiple shades of Capt. Mallory at various points in the film. He accepts the mission because of three character traits—respecting the military tradition of following orders from superiors (as he expects the same from his subordinates), believing in the cause and its 'do-goodness' and having no intention of proving himself as a hero.

Throughout the film, Gregory Peck brings out these aspects perfectly in an understated manner. He talks and exhorts his team only when it is absolutely required. In a brilliant scene towards the movie's climax, even when the grey areas in his character are revealed, he limits his outburst to conveying logic and bringing back focus to the job at hand, rather than giving in to emotion. This, in turn, wins the respect of his detractor in the end.

Focus on the job at hand

> *Miller: You're officially taking command of this team, sir?*
> *Mallory: Yes, I suppose I am. Why?*
> *Miller: Just for the record.*

For Capt. Mallory and team, it is wartime and with a near-fatal mission on hand, the going is never easy. The job has to be completed in less than 6 days, which is further curtailed to 5 days. Moreover, he was never supposed to lead the team in the first place. But he takes it all in his stride and whenever things take an unpredictable turn, he keeps his and the team's focus on the job at hand.

Hold the team together

Miller: I can't swim.

It is always a challenge to lead a team of experts or seasoned professionals. Each one of them brings a certain set of dynamics and idiosyncrasies or as in the case of Col. Andrea Stavros (Anthony Quinn), a strong personal grudge. They also approach the work on hand differently, like the flippant Cpl. John Anthony Miller (David Niven) or brooding CPO 'Butcher' Brown (Stanely Baker). It becomes an important task for Capt. Mallory to set the agenda straight and drive home the priorities. Individuals only see their point of view and their comfort, it is up to the leader to figure the whole mission out.

When things do not go as planned or the team member does not perform as the situation demands, one has to take different approaches to guide or chide them. The movie showcases this brilliantly. When Brown hesitates to kill a German, Mallory observes it but waits for the right time to give the feedback and keeps him away from the main tasks till he learns the importance of it. Mallory employs a different tactic to handle Miller. He ignores his chatter but when the time comes, he gives him a stern order to put together the explosives needed for the job.

> *Mallory: It's our only chance to get the job done. I'm sorry but I couldn't think of any other way.*

Think on one's feet

There is always a plan, to begin with, in any assignment. But things change quickly. The leader has to adapt even more quickly, absorbing it all and in tune with his true nature or self. Gregory Peck presents this very well, true to the character of Mallory. Whenever things go south, he remains the same calculated, focused individual who just wants to get the job done, no matter what. Right from the scene where Franklin is out of action and he has to take over as leader, to the scene before the climax where he has to demand Miller to come out of the wet explosives situation, he doesn't deviate an inch from the character portrayal.

Mallory: You really want your pound of flesh, don't you?

Take tough decisions and act tough, not heroic

How do we define 'tough'? It is when you are convinced that it is the right thing to do, but it is difficult either because of your feelings or that of others. Please note the word 'feelings.' A leader navigates through this terrain, by focusing on logic first and then figuring out ways to make it easy for others or shoving it down their throats when it is the only option.

The toughest decision for Capt. Mallory was to use Major Franklin (Anthony Quayle) as a decoy, especially because he was a good friend. In fact, there is a lovely scene in the boat before it hits the storm where Franklin apologises to Mallory for having dragged him into the assignment along with Stavros. And Mallory brushes it aside.

But Mallory defends his decision towards the end when Miller confronts him and makes a strong case for his action. If he hadn't succeeded, Miller might have gotten away with a mutiny of sorts and jeopardised the mission, if anyone from the team had wavered. He also got ready to kill the lady traitor, as Miller wanted him to. This was a way to get back at him for what he did to Franklin. At the end of it all, it is Mallory'sconviction, true to the character, that saves the day for him and the mission.

Acting tough becomes easy if one internalizes the root of the tough decisions. If deep down, the belief is strong, it manifests appropriately. Mallory does this beautifully with Butcher Brown too and brings him back into the team's main job only when he is mentally ready.

Most important of all, he doesn't get carried away with heroics or take the mission too seriously. It's a job, It's a job, he keeps telling himself and the team and takes it one step at a time. This helps him in two ways—by not being afraid or thinking too much about the perils on the path and by remaining focused on the tasks at hand.

Gregory Peck once again plays his role as the character demands. Be it his usual subdued portrayal or calculated outbursts with Brown and Miller, he is in his element.

When it is over, you move on

When it is all done, as the dust is settling down, leaders reflect on the project briefly and move on to the next. This is very well captured in the movie, in Miller and Mallory's conversation.

> *Miller: To tell you the truth I didn't think we could do it.*
> *Mallory: To tell you the truth neither did I.*

Probably this is the first time that Mallory admits frankly that the mission is beyond their reach. But as Napolean Bonaparte said, "*A leader is a dealer in hope.*" Mallory marches on steadfast and when it is all done, over a puff of smoke, either mulls over his next job or his retirement, leaving the celebrations to the rest. Laurels and heroics seldom interest a true leader.

The same sentiment is expressed in the movie The Untouchables in two scenes. The one where Eliot Ness (Kevin Costner) has had a rough day and meets Malone (Sean Connery) on the way home and the other is at the end when Ness nails Capone. The reporter asks him what he would do if the prohibition is lifted. Here are two great dialogues that sum it up.

Malone: You just fulfilled the first rule of law enforcement: make sure when your shift is over you go home alive. Here endeth the lesson.

* * *

Scoop: Word is they're going to repeal prohibition. What'll you do then?
Ness: [jokingly] I think I'll have a drink.

There are several other films like **Lawrence of Arabia, The Great Escape, Crimson Tide, The Dirty Dozen, The Untouchables, The Bridge on River Kwai,** etc. that not only dwell on various traits of leaders but also different styles of leadership. But what you will find in common are the above-mentioned attributes with the most important of them all, the true character of the leader which is the driving force. Finally, when the job is done, there endeth their involvement.

Process Isn't a Dirty Word

"If you can't describe what you are doing as a process, you don't know what you're doing."

– W. Edwards Deming

If you have had some coding experience, you would learn early on that describing and defining the process is the first step in creating something. The process has an input, some steps and sequences, and the desired output. You keep building many of these and interlink them, and your algorithm evolves. Finally, your master algorithm is a set of processes and sub-processes/procedures that are intended to produce a particular result. However, the word process isn't limited to the programming or software industry. We come across the term in every business, as a part of most of its functions.

What is the advantage of defining such processes and the related procedures/systems? It makes it easy for both novices and seasoned people to carry out certain business-related activities with ease. For instance, in a small firm in the USA that I used to work for, we had a folder with all the standard operating procedures in it, and whenever we had to forward the calls to an agency at the closure of the business we simply followed that procedure step by step. This was our firm's way of not taxing our brains for something as simple as a call forward, which we did occasionally (when the receptionist was not present). It also eased the way for a newbie like me who had just landed in the USA and was still getting used to the work culture. The same book of procedures also had one for a fire alert and what we had to do when the eventuality did occur. It also had various checklists and my all-time favourite was what to do when you were the last person to leave the office. (I would never have switched off the coffee pot otherwise. Without the list, I would have surely contributed to a slim chance of fire due to overheating).

In short, anything and everything can be encapsulated into a process and a set of procedures. When you have them for both routine and rare occurrences, you create a mechanism to continuously improve your business. If NASA can have a set of procedures to service a space shuttle or put one in orbit and vouch for its value, why should we mortals miss out on such a thing? (By the way, I was a part of the team that worked on a program to automate the zillion procedures that go into checking and verifying a certain section of the space shuttle. Phew!)

> *Phil: What would you do if you were stuck in one place and every day was exactly the same, and nothing that you did mattered?*
> *Ralph: That about sums it up for me.*
>
> **– Groundhog Day**

Well, then why is there a resistance to the word 'process' or any adherence to it? Why is it treated like a dirty word on par with any other oft-used ones? Is it because there is a sense that it stifles creativity or curtails individual freedom or is pushed down one's throat without preamble? Or is it because it creates a sense of such a dull routine, that at the end of the day it feels like one's life is not in one's control? Even if all of the above is not accurate, let's see how we can address these.

Clearly define core and non-core processes

Most often, the sheer number of processes put people off. It helps to separate the core and non-core processes and document them accordingly. In many organizations, they are grouped under two types—standard operating procedures and domain/function-specific operating procedures. For instance, if it were a software development outfit, it would become software development procedures and if it were a hospital it would take the form of emergency medical procedures and so on. Once this is done, let the team go through these during the induction process and subsequently increase their familiarity as they go along.

Make them a part of the agenda in team meetings

In weekly meetings, going over one particular process helps everyone stay focused. It might sound boring at times, but the fact that a senior person or the manager, gives his attention to a particular procedure, creates the right kind of importance for it amongst the rest of the team.

Identify and nurture individual process champions, to create a sense of ownership

It is quite likely that certain individuals would develop an affinity toward a specific aspect of the business. It makes great sense to assign them related processes and make them visible champions. For instance, in a digital media outfit, if someone is a stickler for video quality, then making such a person in charge of related processes and procedures works in favour of the individual and the organization.

Review and discard the processes and procedures that are not relevant

Periodic reviews are a must to make sure that any outdated stuff is discarded. For instance, a data backup-related process doesn't make sense if the data is moved to a cloud operation and the entire process is outsourced. Same with a procedure to upload videos to a YouTube channel when the channel no longer exists. Any reviews should be documented, irrespective of a standard like ISO being followed or not.

Make these accessible to everyone

Be it a physical folder or an online repository, the key members of the team must have access to these documents. They should be able to refer to them whenever needed and even give their feedback from time to time.

Yes, deviations are accepted

Finally, the term process is often associated with rigidness, with no scope to deviate even when there is a huge exception. While strict adherence to the processes is a must, one should also be made aware that certain situations warrant a change, especially when the people involved are highly experienced or the stakes are very high. For instance, in the movie **Sully**, the protagonist is forced to break away from the regular procedure when a unique situation at hand demands it. Similarly, there could be situations that actually call for new procedures, like in the movie Apollo 13 where the engineers have to safely bring the astronauts home. Both these cases often led to a new set of procedures and that's how the overall process evolves.

So next time when you are presented with a set of processes/procedures, be mindful that they are for your own good and will work to your advantage.

The only exception could be when you are Luke Skywalker. Remember the last scene in **A New Hope** when the young Luke is urged by Obi Wan to use the Force instead of the computer eye to shoot the target? Unless you can use the Force, may the process be with you.

Drive Your Time

One Armed Man: I've been looking for you for 8 months. Whenever I should have had a gun in my right hand, I thought of you. Now I find you in exactly the position that suits me. I had lots of time to learn to shoot with my left.

(Tuco gets up from the bathtub and shoots him with the hidden gun)
Tuco: When you have to shoot, shoot. Don't talk.

– The Good, the Bad and the Ugly

Not sure if the one-armed man took this great wisdom to his next life, but all of us can take a cue or two from this wonderful scene.

Time is the most valuable commodity in the world and all of us have an equal amount of time in a day. It doesn't matter if you are Einstein or a dud, the time in a single day is the same. It's in our hands as to how we use the 24 hours and do something with it. Most of our squandered chances are actually a result of bad usage of the time at hand. Terms and phrases like opportunity, hard work, smart work, best preparation, making the most of it, etc. are all variants of the usage of time. If we manage our time well, we see results. When we don't, we might risk ending up like the one-armed man.

Sometimes, we have to deal with the perception of time too. For instance, when we are calm and look at nature or a thing of beauty, time appears slower or faster than the actual time elapsed, depending on our involvement and feelings. The same is the case when we are confronting a great danger or a threat when it could feel like minutes are dragging by.

There are theories and stories about how the Samurai trained their mind to either slow up or speed up time at will, to their advantage. This is a bit like Robert McCall (Denzel Washington) in **The Equalizer** who sees everything in slow motion just before an attack.

There is a fundamental difference between how a beginner and an expert look at the flow of time—both real and perceived. While an expert drives time to his advantage, a beginner simply ignores the flow to repent later. We don't have to be like Neo in The Matrix and experience the bullet time aka the matrix effect. It might not be that difficult if we set some ground rules for managing our time. Here are a few.

Your time should reflect what's important to you

> *"The key is not to prioritize what's on your schedule, but to schedule your priorities."*

– Stephen Covey

Our goal should be to spend time on things that are important to us, rather than on things that are thrown at us as being important. Agreed, circumstances do not allow this, but we need to find a way, even if that means having to work longer days. This will turn out to be temporary as we will eventually find a way to strike a balance. We all have to believe in the possibility of spending more time in the second quadrant (important but not urgent), as outlined in the book **The Seven Habits of Highly Effective People** by Stephen Covey.

Believe in the preparation time for any task

> *"Give me six hours to chop down a tree and I will spend the first four sharpening the axe."*

– Abraham Lincoln

Once again we can refer to Stephen Covey and his splitting of time across the four quadrants. The real value lies in the second quadrant because of two reasons. One, if this 'time' is in our control, we can choose to spend it. Two, it is spent on something important but not urgent. This puts us in a good frame of mind to think through all the possibilities and details of the task at hand, without jumping in blindly.

Control the start of the day

"Go ahead, make my day."

– Harry Callahan, Sudden Impact, 1983

We are talking about making a different kind of day here. But the principle is more or less the same. Instead of time staring back at us with a Smith and Wesson, we stare back at it first. What better way to do it than at the start of the day? Whether you are an early riser or not, the first few work hours pretty much decide how your day moves forward. There are examples in the service industry like banks, where the work starts before the business is thrown open to the outside world. It is the same with any counter-based service. A takeaway restaurant will have to prepare first before the counter is activated.

Similarly, in any line of work, we should devote some time at the beginning of the day. This time has to be structured without interruptions in which you either finish a set of tasks (checklists help and work for many top leaders) or use it as a preparatory time for the rest of the day. Once this is done, you can rest assured that you will have enough time for any/all transactional tasks that get pushed onto your plate. You can still have chunks of me-time where you plan or work on important or urgent tasks.

Be frank about time wasters

"I don't waste time with losers, Tommy."

– Andy in The Shawshank Redemption

Often we come across people or tasks which deviate from our regular schedule. We also have a fair idea about them being a waste of time. But we go along either out of obligation or because of our own bad time management. We need to assess every task that we are supposed to do and then decide for or against it. Andy's approach of sizing up Tommy is not a bad idea. But in most cases, we don't have to be that harsh. By simply postponing the request, we will be able to figure out the importance of the task.

I have seen some extreme cases of time management where the bosses do not agree to meet up immediately after the request comes in and even keep skipping or postponing the meeting. They are in a way prioritizing the meeting based on how much the other party is willing to chase them for it! This might work in celebrity-driven domains like media and entertainment or for that matter politics. But in other industries, it is better to use tactics like sticking to a schedule and avoiding deviations and protesting against any changes. This not only puts a price on your time but also gives you a sense of control of your day.

Shift from task to task as if you were meant to be somewhere

> One day Alice came to a fork in the road and saw a Cheshire cat in a tree. *"Which road do I take?"* he asked.
>
> *"Where do you want to go?"* was *his* response.
>
> *"I don't know,"* Alice answered.
>
> *"Then,"* said the cat, *"it doesn't matter."*
>
> **– Alice in Wonderland**

Even when our schedule is not fixed and we have free time on hand, it is always important to conduct and conclude the business at hand to accommodate something else soon after. It doesn't always have to be official stuff. It could be either your personal time (like taking off for a movie, attending a family function, etc.) or time you spend sharpening your axe (reading a book, attending a seminar/session, etc.). The important thing is you get into anything with a definite time frame and a deliverable at the end unless it is a deadline and a war room kind of situation.

An ex-boss of mine would ask his secretary to keep sending small slips about the next meeting (sometimes non-existent) to conclude the current one. So, if you are in a meeting with him, you know your time is over once the slips start showing up. You can devise several other techniques to run a planned schedule, which actually is pretty simple if you have a planned schedule in the first place and the intention to stick to it.

Another ex-boss of mine once told me, that it is always good to walk fast in the corridors, as it dissuades people from having impromptu conversations and also gives them the feeling that you need to get someplace important soon. This is decent advice as long as you don't start walking like Jim Carrey in **Ace Ventura**.

Run a meeting like it has to end

*"Now, if any of you sons of b*****s got ANYTHING ELSE TO SAY, NOW'S THE F*****G TIME!*
[Pause] I didn't think so."

– O-Ren Ishii (Kill Bill Vol.1)

The above dialogue comes soon after a respectable member of the Chinese mafia loses his head when he questions O-Ren Ishii's lineage and her ability to lead the pack. She doesn't say it explicitly, but may be part of the reason for her restlessness was the fact that he was deviating from the agenda.

Sometimes, one has to be mindful about sticking to an agenda or simply put, what gets done in a meeting. Prior to that, one can even question if there is a need for the meeting. Once the need is established, a meeting has to have an agenda, and the entire lot should stick to it. Ultimately, a meeting is not an end in itself as comically shown in a very old Jaspal Bhatti episode on TV.

An example of a more civilized way of running meetings can be taken from The Bridge on the River Kwai. Just after Colonel Saito requests or demands help from Colonel Nicholson to build the bridge, he calls for a meeting. But what he does prior to the meeting is amazing. He surveys the actual site, gets all the latest information about the project by involving the key people and comes very well prepared for the meeting. He drives the meeting with a fixed agenda and deviates with only a few requests here and there, including those for tea and meals.

So, here are a few important things to do before a meeting.

1. Is it necessary as a form of communication in project management?
2. Have we shared all the relevant information with the concerned people?
3. Do we have someone like O-Ren Ishii in the meeting, who will kill if required?
4. Do we have a clear outcome from the meeting other than a confirmation of the next meeting? This is something that Mr. Bhatti points out in his episode.

Maybe a simple thumb rule would be to note how much we have to prepare for a meeting. If it is very important then we ought to prepare like mad and also fight to complete it on time, rather than drop in like flying angels and wait for the show to begin. Once we are clear about the whys and hows of the meetings, we can even knock off many of them.

Execute the day with a purpose

Nurse: Sometimes people just die.
Phil: Not today.

– Groundhog Day

Groundhog day is about Phil Connors, a weatherman stuck in Pennsylvania. He relives the same day over and again. As the (same) day goes by, he comes up with new ways to squander the time, until one day, he sees death at close quarters. An old man he takes to the hospital dies, and he decides to do something about it and vows to himself that he will not die today. Phil undergoes a remarkable transformation from then on and every day he builds up enthusiasm for various 'errands' that he has to take up over and over again. His schedule is choc-a-bloc as he moves from one task to another in an effortless manner.

Having a desire to help others—your kids or parents, or a colleague or best of all, a total stranger—and squeezing related tasks into the day's schedule, gives us a sense of purpose. This motivates us to spend time wisely and execute the day with gusto.

Have a home to go to

Malone: You just fulfilled the first rule of law enforcement: make sure when your shift is over you go home alive. Here endeth the lesson.

– The Untouchables

Believing in a home is the most important thing for any worker. Something to look forward to, someplace to unwind and prepare for the next day. This is as important as getting the daily jobs done. It is sometimes very difficult to switch off from the connected world, but only when we do this, do we re-energize ourselves for the upcoming day.

[Ness has just shot a gangster after the Canadian border raid.]
Ness: I had to kill him.
Malone: Oh, yeah. He's as dead as Julius Caesar… Would you rather it was you?
Ness: No, I would not.
Malone: Well, then, you've done your job. Go home and sleep well tonight.

As Malone (Sean Connery) once again reminds Ness (Kevin Costner), as soon as the job is done, it's time to go home and hit the sack. Rest is the most important task in our daily schedule. Amen!

Appendix

Movies and TV Shows

12 Angry Men

A Bug's Life

A Few Good Men

Ace Ventura

Bad Taste

Bangaru Babu

Breaking Bad

Casino

Crimson Tide

Dirty Dozen

Get Shorty

Groundhog Day

Hoosiers

Indiana Jones and the Last Crusade

Lagaan (Hindi)

Lawrence of Arabia

Mayabazar (Telugu)

Mission Impossible

Ocean's Trilogy

Pirates of Silicon Valley

Sabrina

Scarface

Seinfeld

Seven Samurai (Japanese)

Star Wars

The Bourne Identity

The Bridge on the River Kwai

The Equalizer

The Godfather

The Good, The Bad, The Ugly

The GoodFellas

The Great Escape

The Magnificent Seven

The Matrix

The Shawshank Redemption

The Untouchables

Books

A hero with a Thousand Faces by Joseph Campbell

Alice In Wonderland by Lewis Carroll

Hitchcock's Notebooks: An Authorized And Illustrated Look Inside The Creative Mind Of Alfred Hitchcock by Dan Auiler

Seven Habits of Highly Effective People by Stephen R. Covey

The Circle of Innovation by Tom Peters

The Practice of management by Peter Drucker

What color is your Parachute? by Richard Nelson Bolles

Index